MUSIC
AN APPRECIATION
FIFTH BRIEF EDITION

BY ROGER KAMIEN

MULTIMEDIA COMPANION CD-ROM 5.0

A clear, concise explanation of how to use the tools found on the CD-ROM.

Mc Graw Hill

Boston   Burr Ridge, IL   Dubuque, IA   Madison, WI   New York
San Francisco   St. Louis   Bangkok   Bogotá   Caracas   Kuala Lumpur
Lisbon   London   Madrid   Mexico City   Milan   Montreal   New Delhi
Santiago   Seoul   Singapore   Sydney   Taipei   Toronto

GETTING STARTED

WINDOWS	MACINTOSH
1. Insert disk, "Multimedia Companion 5.0 CD-ROM," into your CD-ROM drive. 2. Click on the Start Button on the bottom left of your desktop and select Run. 3. Type D:\ (or letter of your CD-ROM drive). 4. Double-click the "Start_Here.exe" file.	1. Insert disk, "Multimedia Companion 5.0 CD-ROM," into your CD-ROM drive. 2. Double-click on the CD-ROM icon, which will say Kamien CD. 3. Double-click the "Start Here" file.

Following these instructions for Windows and Macintosh will launch your browser and you can begin using the program. If your browser does not launch, see the Read_Me.txt on the CD-ROM for more information.

MINIMUM SYSTEM REQUIREMENTS

WINDOWS

* Pentium IV (or equivalent) or better recommended with 256 MB RAM or higher
* Windows 98SE or higher (Windows XP or later recommended)
* CD-ROM drive
* Sound Blaster or compatible sound card
* Sound settings that enable the use of headphones or speakers
* Internet connection (to use a portion of this product)
* XGA 16bit color monitor, 1024 x 768 resolution

MACINTOSH

* PowerMac with 256 MB RAM or higher. G3 or G4 processor recommended
* MacOS 9.2 or higher (MacOS X 10.2 or higher recommended)
* CD-ROM drive
* External speakers or headphones
* Internet connection (to use a portion of this product)
* XGA 16bit color monitor, 1024 x 768 resolution

TECHNICAL SUPPORT

www.mhhe.com/support

If you have any questions or experience any difficulties using this CD-ROM, please use our customer support Web site located at www.mhhe.com/support.

MADE WITH macromedia®

A QUICK OVERVIEW

The Multimedia Companion is designed to make your study of music easier, more rewarding, and more fun. The material found on this CD-ROM will help you to understand basic concepts, test your knowledge, and listen to music more effectively.

The CD-ROM opens to a brief Overview section explaining the contents of the software. To go directly to the content of the CD-ROM, use the pull-down menus at the top of the screen.

Music An Appreciation by Roger Kamien   Intro   Elements   Instruments   Listening   Opera   Activities   Resources

The **Intro** Section will help familiarize you with all that the CD-ROM has to offer. In addition to *System Requirements* and *Credits*, this section provides a *Music Appreciation Primer* that includes an informative series of answers to questions that students who are new to the study of music will appreciate.

The **Elements** section of the CD-ROM provides enhanced explanations, activities, and quizzes that relate to Part I ("Elements") in your text.

The **Instruments** section contains *Video Demonstrations*, an *Instrument Lab*, and an interactive version of Britten's *The Young Person's Guide to the Orchestra*.

The **Listening** section contains software that provides interactive versions of the Listening Outlines in the text as well as additional recordings and "New Horizons in Music Appreciation."

The **Opera** section contains video excerpts of three operas, all of which directly correlate to discussions in the text.

The **Activities** menu contains a fun and interactive way for students to listen to and gain a better understanding of some of the common forms heard in concert settings. Activities are provided for *Concerto Grosso*, *Fugue*, *Minuet*, *Sonata*, *Rondo*, and *Theme and Variations*.

The **Resources** section contains additional tools of interest such as *Interactive Timelines*, *The Concert-Goer's Guide*, a *Multimedia Glossary*, and a link to the *Online Learning Center* for the text.

ELEMENTS OF MUSIC

A fully interactive Elements section provides visual and audio examples of the concepts covered in Part I of your textbook. The appropriate chapter number for whichever version of the Kamien text you are using is noted at the top of each page for easy reference. In addition to textual summaries of important concepts, animated demonstration activities allow you to directly experience musical elements in action.

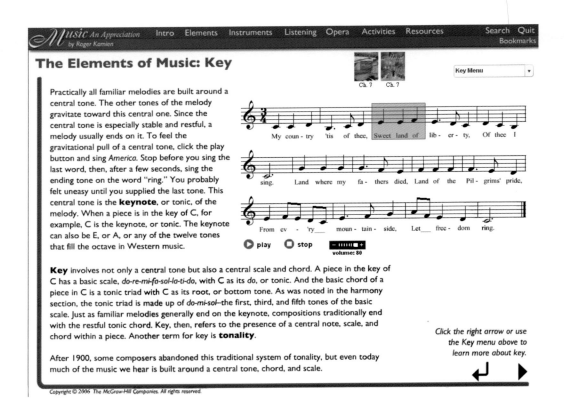

Where applicable, musical scores are presented along with an audio clip.

At the end of each section, a quiz assesses your grasp of the material. Detailed results pages are provided along with the answers. The quiz results can be e-mailed to your professor.

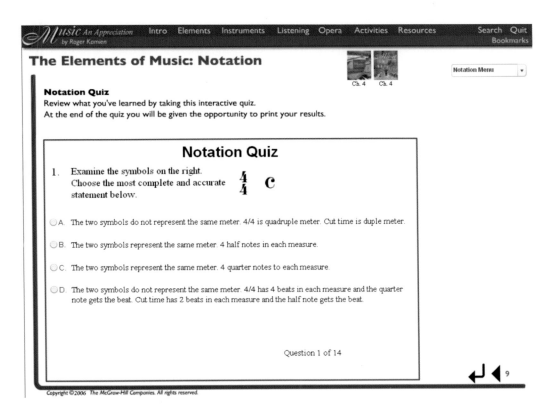

INSTRUMENTS

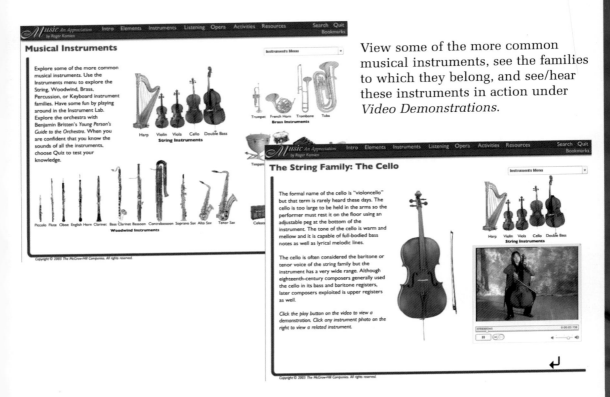

View some of the more common musical instruments, see the families to which they belong, and see/hear these instruments in action under *Video Demonstrations*.

Also, visit the *Instrument Lab*, an interactive area where you can hear the sounds made by unique instruments by using your computer keyboard (not pictured here).

Benjamin Britten's *The Young Person's Guide to the Orchestra* is provided in an interactive format. This allows you to select different sections of the orchestra and listen to the music of each one at any time.

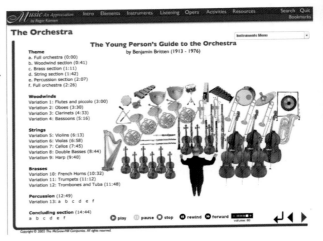

LISTENING

The Kamien **Listening Outlines** in the text are presented in a dynamic format called *ChartPlayer*, created by Larry Worster. This software turns your computer into an interactive listening station, enabling you to navigate through each musical selection with ease. A link to the software is provided on this CD-ROM.

The music is accompanied by written narration that is coordinated to the music. No more confusing CD timings and tracks-just click, listen, and enjoy!

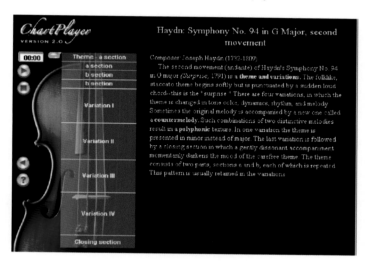

Also contained under the **Listening** menu are numerous *Additional Recordings* of works by composers who are mentioned in the text. In addition, you can listen to Peter Schickele's *New Horizons in Music Appreciation*, which offers an amusing, tongue-in-cheek appreciation of the first movement of Beethoven's Fifth Symphony. This piece broadcasts the performance as if it were a sporting event, complete with play-by-play analysis and color commentary of the "battle" between conductor and musicians!

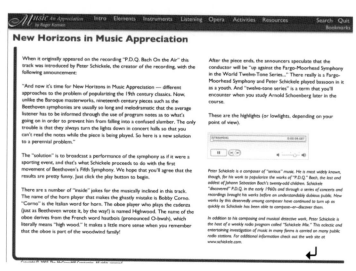

BRINGING OPERA TO LIFE

The **Opera** menu contains forty minutes of video excerpts from three of the operas studied in the text. All excerpts directly correspond to the scenes of the opera discussed in the text and illustrated with Vocal Music Guides. The high-quality video features digital stereo sound with English subtitles. A complete synopsis of each opera is also provided. These opera video excerpts are courtesy of RM Associates.

RM ASSOCIATES

Don Giovanni (Mozart)

Zürich Opera with Nikolaus Harnoncourt conducting. Rodney Gilfrey (Don Giovanni), László Polgár (Leporello), Isabel Rey (Donna Anna), Cecilia Bartoli (Donna Elvira), Liliana Nikiteanu (Zerlina), and Matti Salminen (Commendatore).

Act I: Opening scene from orchestral introduction through the death of the Commendatore, concluding with Leporello's line "Non vo' nulla, signor, non parlo piu." Approx. 6 minutes (pp. 183-186 in text).

Act I: Leporello's "Catalogue" aria ("Madamina"). Approx. 4 minutes (pp. 186-188 in text).

Act I: Duet: "La ci darem la mano." Approx. 2:15 (not in text; Hardcover: pp. 237-239 in text).

La Bohème (Puccini)

Luciano Pavarotti and Mirella Freni star in a live recording of this well-regarded production from the San Francisco Opera conducted by Tiziano Severini. Captured in their primes, Pavarotti and Freni "turned in incandescent performances as Puccini's young lovers" according to the *San Francisco Times*.

Act I: Excerpt from "Non sono in vena" through the end of Act I. Approx. 17 minutes (pp. 271-275 in text] [NOTE: brief text excerpt ends after Rodolfo's aria, approx. 7 minutes].

Wozzeck (Berg)

Recorded under studio conditions from the stage of the Frankfurter Oper. Frankfurter Museumsorchester and Choir, Children's Choir of the Franfurter Oper with Peter Mussbach conducting. Dale Duesing (Wozzeck), Dieter Bundschuh (Captain), Frode Olsen (Doctor), and Kristine Ciesinski (Marie).

This highly stylized production emphasizes the emotional intensity of the work.

Act III, Scenes 4-5: the conclusion of the opera. Approx. 8:30 (pp. 327-330 in text).

ACTIVITIES

The **Activities** menu contains six game-like exercises to help solidify your understanding of a few of the common forms heard in concert settings.

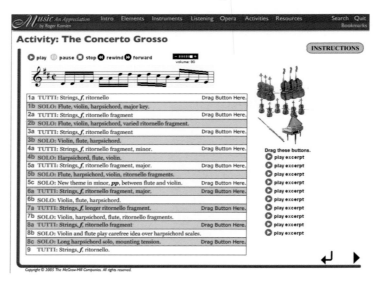

Matching exercises use click-and-drag technology and help tune your ear to the different forms, while the works can be "viewed" in animated musical scores. Activities are provided for *Concerto Grosso*, *Fugue*, *Minuet*, *Sonata*, *Rondo*, and *Theme and Variations*.

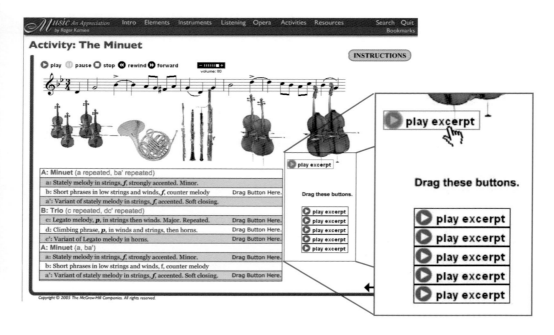

RESOURCES

Presented here are six *Interactive Timelines* that present an in-depth and informative view of specific time periods. Important events are noted in music, arts and letters, and history. Audio examples relevant to the specific time period are also included, along with a selection of artwork from each period.

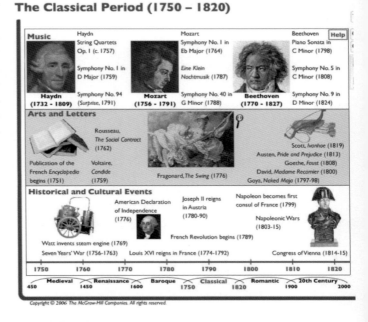

Also under the **Resources** menu, the *Multimedia Glossary* is included in an easy-to-use format. Audio examples of musical terms are provided, where applicable.

You'll find the *Concert-Goer's Guide* and a direct link to the text's *Online Learning Center* under the **Resources** menu as well. These tools will help you to better understand and enjoy concert performances, provide tips for writing concert reports, and link you to the wealth of additional material found on the OLC, including quizzes and chapter summaries.